# ALFRED LESLIE

# 100 VIEWS ALONG THE ROAD

TIMKEN PUBLISHERS, INC · NEW YORK

# OUR LUMINOUS PARADISE

A variety of steps led up to these watercolors, but a disaster I suppose set it all off. On October 17, 1966, my studio-home burned and twelve New York City firefighters died. I was shocked by their deaths and devastated by my personal loss of nearly everything that I owned. Gone were all the new figurative paintings I had ready for a one-man show at the Whitney Museum. Lost was the new film I had just screened for the selection committee at the Lincoln Center Film Festival. My entire life's work as artist was in a shambles and I was left with my five-year-old son, no savings, no insurance, many acquaintances and a few good friends. Two of them provided me with a temporary bed, a few others began a fund for my financial relief, and I got grants from three foundations to help me start life over. With so much lost, mourning was impossible, so in a month's time I was working again in a new studio. One of the first projects I began was *The Killing Cycle*, a series of paintings I had planned before the fire. Not surprisingly, death was the subject.

The following summer I rented a bay-front cottage in Easthampton, Long Island, to make some landscape watercolor studies for *The Killing Cycle* project. I concentrated on light and atmosphere, painting skies mostly, with small bits of water and beach. I also eliminated color in favor of grisaille as I had done in my earlier work. At the end of that summer, after I had made about thirty of these watercolors, I realized they had emerged so strongly as an independent group that they were competing with *The Killing Cycle* for my attention. To prevent this, I put them away so I could complete *The Killing Cycle* first. But it was well over a decade before that would happen, and ironically, another crisis was needed to jolt me into summoning those watercolors back.

It was a fine spring day in 1978 and I was returning from California, where I had spent ten wasted weeks trying to develop a group of landscape paintings. I was in my Ford van, heading east outside Laguna, New Mexico. The van was swaying in a strong crosswind from the heap of stuff piled high on the roof rack, so high that I had taped a sign on the dashboard that said: "11 FEET, 7 INCHES." I was hitting about eighty when a car passed me on the right. The driver beeped the horn and pointed up. I reached through the window to check the lines that were the extra tie-downs for the rack. They were gone. I pulled off the road. Frayed rope ends hung down like the dreadlocks of a Rastafarian. The load was about to fall. Some lamp shades were already gone, and I certainly had had more two-by-fours. I carefully took everything else down and kept only what would fit inside the van. I felt kind of good. I hated that stuff anyway. It reminded me of those awful landscapes I had just painted in Santa Barbara and the ten frustrating weeks of daily foot-slogging burdened with the gear of an itinerant scene painter. I kept on driving. The day seemed endless. My abandoned furniture finally vanished from the rear view mirror and was replaced by white lines.

I was regretting the whole trip when a singular pile of colossal stones came into view. Gargantuan stones lying helter-skelter as if they had been casually crumpled by Goya's mad mammoth just before he began to stuff those screaming babies into his mouth. At the base of the rocks were scattered a few trailers. All this was backlit with a pellucid light in the manner of an epiphany. This sublime western scene hit me hard and interested me more than anything I had just painted in California. I knew I could rescue my trip from failure by drawing it.

The gods were definitely in control, and they had left a drawing pad and 4B pencil clearly visible in the jumbled mess behind the seat.

I pulled off the road again, this time to draw a series of four rectangles on a page, one under the other like a vertical cartoon on about twenty sheets. I turned back about five miles and made another run at the site. This time as I approached I didn't stop. Instead, I pressed my knees against the bottom of the steering wheel and began to draw. I managed a few hasty scribbles and filled in one of the long rectangular boxes with a landscape that was really a succession of views. Since I was not drawing from any fixed position, the landscape sketch became a composite of many angles. They would all merge, making the final drawing a compound of individual sightings. Instead of Duchamp's *Nude Descending a Staircase*, a painted sequence of stop-motion images all on one canvas, I had condensed a hundred separate percepts into one view. Landscape as myth.

I liked what I did with that sketch and drew from the speeding van all the way back east to my Massachusetts studio. I called them my driving drawings. But once home I didn't know what to do with them, so I put them all away and tacked up the dreadful watercolors from Santa Barbara. I tried reworking the watercolors that whole spring and summer. Then very late one balmy fall night, I realized the California pictures were a dead end and I had to move on.

The driving drawings were out of my mind for nearly two years when I recollected them again. I had gone for a ride in my old Volvo. I wasn't going anywhere specific. I just wanted to saunter on wheels, to clear my head, to think. But I didn't go very far and parked at the local Stop & Shop in Hadley. It was about 3 A.M. by now and there was a thin sliver of moon crisply stated in the sky. On impulse I sat in a small square of grass in the middle of the asphalt parking lot where a tree was planted. Looking up, I noticed an Exxon sign poised high on a tall mast, like another moon. I thought how similar all this was to the scene outside Laguna with the trailers parked underneath those gigantic ancient rocks. Then as now, everything seemed timeless, steeped in calm, without people and faintly doomed.

I went back to my studio and pulled out the drawings I had done of that Laguna view, then retrieved those black-and-white watercolors I had done even earlier in Easthampton for *The Killing Cycle*, the watercolors I had put away so long before because it wasn't the right time to pursue them. It occurred to me then to combine them. The driving drawings of just snips and pieces of signs, roads, trees and mountains could become the foregrounds for those monochromatic skies of the watercolors. It was a beginning.

First, I reviewed the formal basis of the watercolors, starting with the white band that was at the bottom of every picture. I had discovered the band accidentally, after removing the tape I used to mask off sections of paper. When I saw the band for the first time I realized that the white unpainted section of the paper not only looked beautiful, but also provided a simultaneous second reading of the picture. It told the viewer that the painted sky above the white band was paint and nothing more. In this seeming subversion of pictorial realism and naturalness, the white band also functioned as a signifier, signing the wholeness of nature. Its role was similar to the fast gradation of intense blue at the very top of Japanese prints that indicates sky directly overhead, which you cannot see without looking up but you know is there as you are looking straight ahead at the horizon. As that intense blue signifies sky out of sight, my white band stands for earth not in view but as a given. The ground you know you are standing on as you look ahead. Earth as ground, ground as ground, base, surface of the paper. Its conceptual function, though, began with an entirely eyeball pleasure. I liked it, identified it, asked what it might mean, and kept it. The white band both signifies and is.

The white band was also the natural yield of my thoughts about making the sketches with a monochromatic palette limited to black thinned with water. My grisaille would stand for all color. Continuing my past work, I used black as a color, not its absence; black as the carrier of light, not its executioner. My strictures: no color but a

TRailer S    outside Laguna NM on 40

single black, one size paper, one brush. Simple materials that would not blur the idea of the pictures. For most people reality is the confirmation of their expectations. These pictures would offer alternatives. Minimal means and probity would link the mind and the eye. I intended to use similar ideas for inventing landscape that I had used for inventing people in the paintings lost in the fire of 1966. In those paintings people became moral equations, lit by ideas in the guise of forty-watt bulbs. Now natural light was the bridge. As I had done before the fire, I would eliminate all esthetic choices in favor of pure information. I would resist meaning and interpretation. I would paint with nature rather than from nature. I would be nature.

Nature and process, then, were the formal imperatives for the watercolors. But I was helped further in the definition of these ideas by the fortuitous discovery of the Japanese concept of *nōtan*, in a Chinese library on Essex Street in New York City. The concept is based on the belief that there can be an eternal unchanging response to the certain beauty of just so much white to just so much black.

*Nōtan* has no counterpart in English and was brought into the vocabulary of English-speaking artists by the painter Arthur Dow in his book *Composition*, published in 1899. The word is both descriptive and judgmental, bespeaking both style and quality. It is a noun and an adjective. I called the original pictures Notans.

The first tests of the black washes I laid down after I had reviewed all my formal equations were dismal failures. For black, uncommon in the practice of watercolor altogether, is notoriously hard to manage. The earlier watercolors, being only sky, never required the very bottom range of black. I had to succeed here if I was to go ahead. I selected a favored composition to start with, that trailer site with the sobering rocks that had surprised me outside Laguna. I kept painting that composition for two months until I made one that satisfied me, and discovered as well the method I would pursue until the end of the series.

I reproduced one of the drawings on ten or so sheets of watercolor paper that had been soaked, stretched and dried. I used sable lettering on the gray scale. The camera records a systematic truth, not a perceptual one. I have translated the original color sensation into a value pattern that is parallel to the original sighting. For example, a red road sign seen against a backdrop of a light blue sky might read through a gray-scaled photographic accounting as black against a light gray. I would offer a white sign against a darker sky. In this instance the complete reversal of the photographic value contrast is truer to the original viewing. I reach to respond to the original sensation of color.

I have also separated these works from photographic practice in that none of the pictures is anecdotal or topographical. My truth to the site is movement, atmosphere and especially light. Light is one of my primary goals and I have used different ways to achieve that in these works. One is to let the details yield to breadth. Another is to help express light by alluding to time and movement. Events of light, depicted sequentially, express transience. These transitions of light are nature stories. But the light I paint is paint, not light. And I remind the viewer that we are looking at pictures, looking at paint, by occasionally pasting moons or road signs on the paper and by leaving staple marks and paint runs visible. I like to have the surface of the paper physically reaffirmed. And I am keen on the abrupt, purposeful transition from fused atmospheric passages to the crisp geometric forms on the surface of the picture.

In 1983, with many of the largest works nearly done, despite paper problems, hallucinations and the clamor of the everyday, I still needed one more clue for the completion of the one hundred pictures, a final title. Naming here was not extrapictorial. It was another formal element, a structural decision as important as the pictorial scheme and the storytelling. *One Hundred Views* had been my working title but I needed something that referred to a car and the road. The title then became *100 Views Along the Road*. With the naming, the structured event that the narrative had become fell into place, not through prior calculation but through growth fed by chance and sensibility. The

pictures were individually about light and atmosphere. As a totality, though, they were about being on the road, in the fast lane, not about this or that place, dawn or night, rain or snow, so much as about being in a car going. Where one got to, what one saw, was subordinated to being on the move. Almost as important as the individual works themselves was the mise-en-scène, the flavor not of the sandwiches that were packed but the packing, not of the money spent on gas but the leaning against the car at the pump when the tank was being filled, not the food in the diner but the driving into the vision of the place. By trying to be true to and distinguishing between the important and subtle differences in seeing from a car rather than on foot, I was declaring the real boundary that I thought set these works apart from simple souvenir paintings of a trip across the country. Anecdotal souvenir pictures were what I had been bringing back from California. Those were the works I hated and rejected and that were so troubling to me when I dumped all my stuff in the desert and first saw the Holy Land in the guise of a few trailers at the foot of those towering boulders.

There are no people in these pictures, no cars or trains, no planes or garbage cans. And there are just a few pictures with buildings. But there are plenty of paintings with bright movie screens and glowing road signs, accents that stamp directions into the night for travelers and set off horizons, trees and moons over glittering ponds. Yet outside that highway furniture there is nothing really to tell us when this narrative took place. Still, I think it looks distinctly of its time—this story that takes place in a car, the getting in, the buckling up and driving, the getting out to pee, to stretch and eat, then the getting back in and starting again, driving along across the country, locked into a tin box and looking out at our luminous paradise.

ALFRED LESLIE
1988

1  APPROACHING GALLUP, NEW MEXICO

2  HOLYOKE RANGE, NEAR OXBOW, EASTHAMPTON, MASSACHUSETTS

3-9  RAINBOW NEAR HADLEY, MASSACHUSETTS

11-14  PAINTED DESERT, ARIZONA

15–18  HEADING FOR GALLUP, NEW MEXICO

19  APPROACHING SPRINGFIELD, MASSACHUSETTS

20　VIEW FROM CASA COYOTE, SANTA BARBARA, CALIFORNIA

21  TOWARDS MT. SUGARLOAF, DEERFIELD, MASSACHUSETTS

22  TURNOFF, HOLYOKE, MASSACHUSETTS

23-24  SALTWATER POND, EASTHAMPTON, LONG ISLAND, NEW YORK

25–29  ROCKY BEACH, SANTA BARBARA, CALIFORNIA

30 DUNES OUTSIDE PROVINCETOWN, MASSACHUSETTS

31–33  OUTSIDE LAGUNA, NEW MEXICO

34–37  OUTSIDE BLUE WATER VILLAGE, NEW MEXICO

38–45  DRIVE-IN MOVIE, SANTA BARBARA, CALIFORNIA

46–49  WINSLOW, ARIZONA

50–51 DRIFTING SNOW ON THE MASS PIKE

52  FULL MOON AND RISING SUN NEAR TULSA, OKLAHOMA

53  PARKING LOT IN DOWNTOWN TULSA, OKLAHOMA

54  FOUR SIGNS, TULSA, OKLAHOMA

55–60  NEAR GALLUP, NEW MEXICO

63–68  APPROACHING THE GRAND CANYON

69-70  HORIZON AT SANTA BARBARA, CALIFORNIA

71–75   ROUTE 116, TOWARDS HADLEY, MASSACHUSETTS

76  SNOW DRIFTING OVER OLD ROAD CUTS, NEW LONDON, CONNECTICUT

78  VIEW OF MEANDER RESERVOIR, YOUNGSTOWN, OHIO

79 ORCHARD CRATES, SANTA BARBARA, CALIFORNIA

80–85  BRIDGE FROM MILL CREEK PARK, YOUNGSTOWN, OHIO

86  OUTSIDE BEAVER, PENNSYLVANIA

87  NEAR AUSTINTOWN PLAZA, YOUNGSTOWN, OHIO

88  BILLBOARDS NEAR OLYMPIA RINK, SPRINGFIELD, MASSACHUSETTS

89  INTERSECTION ON BELMONT AVENUE, YOUNGSTOWN, OHIO

90   AUSTINTOWN PLAZA, YOUNGSTOWN, OHIO

91-92  NORTH SIDE DRIVE-IN THEATER, BELMONT AVENUE AND GYPSY LANE, YOUNGSTOWN, OHIO

93   NEW ASPHALT IN AMHERST, MASSACHUSETTS

94  INTO NEW LONDON, CONNECTICUT

95   OLD SNOW NEAR WATCH HILL, RHODE ISLAND

96   ROUTE 11 WEST OF YOUNGSTOWN, OHIO

97  VIEW OVER HOLYOKE, MASSACHUSETTS

98–100  COAL PILE NEAR THE OHIO RIVER

# EXHIBITIONS OF THE WATERCOLORS

Oil and Steel Gallery, New York, New York
OCTOBER 26–DECEMBER 3, 1983

Worcester Museum of Fine Art, Worcester, Massachusetts
FEBRUARY 15–APRIL 2, 1984

Butler Institute of American Art, Youngstown, Ohio
APRIL 13–MAY 27, 1984

Wichita Art Museum, Wichita, Kansas
JUNE 17–JULY 22, 1984

Newport Harbor Art Museum, Newport Beach California
FEBRUARY 7–MARCH 24, 1985

Henry Art Gallery, University of Washington, Seattle, Washington
APRIL 3–MAY 26, 1985

Philbrook Art Center, Tulsa, Oklahoma
JUNE 30–SEPTEMBER 15, 1985

Rahr-West Museum and Civic Center, Manitowoc, Wisconsin
SEPTEMBER 29–OCTOBER 27, 1985

# LIST OF WATERCOLORS

1 Approaching Gallup, New Mexico, 1978/81, 30″ × 42″

2 Holyoke Range, near Oxbow, Easthampton, Massachusetts, 1983, 44½″ × 45″

3 Rainbow near Hadley, Massachusetts, 1983, 18″ × 24″
4 Rainbow near Hadley, Massachusetts, 1983, 18″ × 24″
5 Rainbow near Hadley, Massachusetts, 1983, 18″ × 24″
6 Rainbow near Hadley, Massachusetts, 1983, 18″ × 24″
7 Rainbow near Hadley, Massachusetts, 1983, 18″ × 24″
8 Rainbow near Hadley, Massachusetts, 1983, 18″ × 24″
9 Rainbow near Hadley, Massachusetts, 1983, 18″ × 24″

10 Route 116, near Sunderland, Massachusetts, 1983, 44″ × 58″

11 Painted Desert, Arizona, 1978/81, 18″ × 24″
12 Painted Desert, Arizona, 1978/81, 18″ × 24″
13 Painted Desert, Arizona, 1978/81, 18″ × 24″
14 Painted Desert, Arizona, 1978/81, 18″ × 24″

15 Heading for Gallup, New Mexico, 1978/81, 18″ × 24″
16 Heading for Gallup, New Mexico, 1978/81, 18″ × 24″
17 Heading for Gallup, New Mexico, 1978/81, 18″ × 24″
18 Heading for Gallup, New Mexico, 1978/81, 18″ × 24″

19 Approaching Springfield, Massachusetts, 1983, 44″ × 57″

20 View from Casa Coyote, Santa Barbara, California, 1978/83, 44″ × 60″

21 Towards Mt. Sugarloaf, Deerfield, Massachusetts, 1983, 44″ × 59″

22 Turnoff, Holyoke, Massachusetts, 1983, 40″ × 60″

23 Saltwater Pond, Easthampton, Long Island, New York, 1978/83, 18″ × 24″
24 Saltwater Pond, Easthampton, Long Island, New York, 1978/83, 18″ × 24″

25 Rocky Beach, Santa Barbara, California, 1978/81, 40″ × 60″
26 Rocky Beach, Santa Barbara, California, 1978/83, 18″ × 24″
27 Rocky Beach, Santa Barbara, California, 1978/83, 18″ × 24″
28 Rocky Beach, Santa Barbara, California, 1978/83, 18″ × 24″
29 Rocky Beach, Santa Barbara, California, 1978/83, 18″ × 24″

30 Dunes outside Provincetown, Massachusetts, 1983, 44″ × 59″

31 Outside Laguna, New Mexico, 1978/81, 30″ × 42″
32 Outside Laguna, New Mexico, 1978/81, 30″ × 42″
33 Outside Laguna, New Mexico, 1978/81, 30″ × 42″

34 Outside Blue Water Village, New Mexico, 1978/81, 18″ × 24″
35 Outside Blue Water Village, New Mexico, 1978/81, 18″ × 24″
36 Outside Blue Water Village, New Mexico, 1978/81, 18″ × 24″
37 Outside Blue Water Village, New Mexico, 1978/81, 18″ × 24″

38 Drive-In Movie, Santa Barbara, California, 1978/81, 30″ × 42″
39 Drive-In Movie, Santa Barbara, California, 1978/81, 18″ × 24″
40 Drive-In Movie, Santa Barbara, California, 1978/81, 18″ × 24″
41 Drive-In Movie, Santa Barbara, California, 1978/81, 18″ × 24″
42 Drive-In Movie, Santa Barbara, California, 1978/81, 18″ × 24″
43 Drive-In Movie, Santa Barbara, California, 1978/81, 18″ × 24″
44 Drive-In Movie, Santa Barbara, California, 1978/81, 18″ × 24″
45 Drive-In Movie, Santa Barbara, California, 1978/81, 30″ × 42″

46 Winslow, Arizona, 1978/81, 18″ × 24″
47 Winslow, Arizona, 1978/81, 18″ × 24″
48 Winslow, Arizona, 1978/81, 18″ × 24″
49 Winslow, Arizona, 1978/81, 18″ × 24″

50 Drifting Snow on the Mass Pike, 1983, 18″ × 24″
51 Drifting Snow on the Mass Pike, 1983, 18″ × 24″

52 Full Moon and Rising Sun near Tulsa, Oklahoma, 1978/81, 18″ × 24″

53 Parking Lot in Downtown Tulsa, Oklahoma, 1981/83, 41″ × 55½″

54 Four Signs, Tulsa, Oklahoma, 1981/83, 45″ × 60″

55 Near Gallup, New Mexico, 1978/81, 30″ × 42″
56 Near Gallup, New Mexico, 1978/81, 18″ × 24″
57 Near Gallup, New Mexico, 1978/81, 18″ × 24″
58 Near Gallup, New Mexico, 1978/81, 18″ × 24″
59 Near Gallup, New Mexico, 1978/81, 18″ × 24″
60 Near Gallup, New Mexico, 1978/81, 30″ × 42″

61 Entering 91 at Holyoke, Massachusetts, 1983, 18″ × 24″
62 Entering 91 at Holyoke, Massachusetts, 1983, 18″ × 24″

63 Approaching the Grand Canyon, 1978/81, 30″ × 42″
64 Approaching the Grand Canyon, 1978/81, 18″ × 24″
65 Approaching the Grand Canyon, 1978/81, 18″ × 24″
66 Approaching the Grand Canyon, 1978/81, 18″ × 24″
67 Approaching the Grand Canyon, 1978/81, 18″ × 24″
68 Approaching the Grand Canyon, 1978/81, 18″ × 24″

69 Horizon at Santa Barbara, California, 1978/81, 30″ × 42″
70 Horizon at Santa Barbara, California, 1978/81, 30″ × 43½″

71 Route 116 towards Hadley, Massachusetts, 1983, 18″ × 24″
72 Route 116 towards Hadley, Massachusetts, 1983, 18″ × 24″
73 Route 116 towards Hadley, Massachusetts, 1983, 18″ × 24″
74 Route 116 towards Hadley, Massachusetts, 1983, 18″ × 24″
75 Route 116 towards Hadley, Massachusetts, 1983, 18″ × 24″

76 Snow Drifting over Old Road Cuts, New London, Connecticut, 1983, 44″ × 59″

77 Drifting Snow near Boston Harbor, 1983, 18″ × 24″

78 View of Meander Reservoir, Youngstown, Ohio, 1983, 18″ × 24″

79 Orchard Crates, Santa Barbara, California, 1978/83, 44″ × 59″

80  Bridge from Mill Creek Park, Youngstown, Ohio, 1983, 44″ × 59″
81  Bridge from Mill Creek Park, Youngstown, Ohio, 1983, 18″ × 24″
82  Bridge from Mill Creek Park, Youngstown, Ohio, 1983, 18″ × 24″
83  Bridge from Mill Creek Park, Youngstown, Ohio, 1983, 18″ × 24″
84  Bridge from Mill Creek Park, Youngstown, Ohio, 1983, 18″ × 24″
85  Bridge from Mill Creek Park, Youngstown, Ohio, 1983, 18″ × 24″

86  Outside Beaver, Pennsylvania, 1983, 44½″ × 59″

87  Near Austintown Plaza, Youngstown, Ohio, 1983, 18″ × 24″

88  Billboards near Olympia Rink, Springfield, Massachusetts, 1983, 18″ × 24″

89  Intersection on Belmont Avenue, Youngstown, Ohio, 1983, 18″ × 24″

90  Austintown Plaza, Youngstown, Ohio, 1983, 18″ × 24″

91  North Side Drive-In Theater, Belmont Avenue and Gypsy Lane, Youngstown, Ohio, 1983, 18″ × 24″
92  North Side Drive-In Theater, Belmont Avenue and Gypsy Lane, Youngstown, Ohio, 1983, 44″ × 59″

93  New Asphalt in Amherst, Massachusetts, 1983, 44½ × 59½″

94  Into New London, Connecticut, 1983, 36″ × 53″

95  Old Snow near Watch Hill, Rhode Island, 1983, 36″ × 53″

96  Route 11, west of Youngstown, Ohio, 1983, 36″ × 53″

97  View over Holyoke, Massachusetts, 1983, 36″ × 53″

98  Coal Pile near the Ohio River, 1983, 44″ × 59″
99  Coal Pile near the Ohio River, 1983, 18″ × 24″
100  Coal Pile near the Ohio River, 1983, 18″ × 24″

Library of Congress Cataloging-in-Publication Data

Leslie, Alfred, 1927–
    100 views along the road/Alfred Leslie.
        p.     cm.
    ISBN 0-943221-01-3
        1. Leslie, Alfred, 1927–     .    2. United States in art.     I. Title.
    II. Title: One hundred views along the road.
    ND1839.L42A4      1988                 88-12391 CIP
    759.13—dc19

Printed in the United States of America

## PHOTOGRAPH CREDITS

Frontispiece, numbers 1–11, 13, 16–17, 19–22, 24–25, 27–32, 38–39, 41–42, 45, 50–58, 61–64, 66–67, 69–75, 77–92, 98–100 by Stephen Petegorsky, Northampton, Massachusetts; numbers 12, 14–15, 18, 23, 26, 33–37, 40, 43–44, 46–49, 59–60, 65, 68, 76, 93–97 by Steven Sloman, New York, New York

100 Views Along the Road

HAS BEEN PRINTED IN AN EDITION OF 3500 COPIES
AT MERIDEN-STINEHOUR PRESS.
MONOTYPE COMPOSITION BY A. COLISH, INC.
DESIGN BY JANE TIMKEN AND JERRY KELLY

1988